Cherry Blossoms at the Tidal Basin

Washington, D.C. Photos

By S. Floyd Mori

Cherry Blossom at the Tidal Basin

Washington, D.C. Photos

About the Author

S. Floyd Mori is an American of Japanese heritage. He was born and raised in Utah. After graduating from high school, he joined the United States Army Reserves. He started college at the University of Southern California (USC), and he served a two-year mission to Hawaii for the Church or Jesus Christ of Latter-day Saints (Mormon). He received a Bachelors and a Masters Degree from Brigham Young University (BYU) with an emphasis on Economics, Asian Studies, and Political Science.

He is the President/CEO of the Asian Pacific American Institute for Congressional Studies (APAICS) in Washington, D.C. APAICS is a national non-partisan, non-profit organization dedicated to promoting Asian Pacific American participation and representation at all levels of the political process from community service to elective office.

He has been the National Executive Director/CEO of the Japanese American Citizens League (JACL), the oldest and largest Asian American civil and human rights organization in the United States. He was also President and Vice President on the National Board of the JACL. A major focus of the JACL is civil rights.

Previously, he taught Economics at Chabot College in Hayward, California, for ten years and served in the California State Assembly for six years. He was Mayor and City Councilman of the City of Pleasanton, California. He has been a Businessman and an International Business Consultant.

He has spoken and written extensively about civil rights and the Japanese American experience of World War II when 120,000 persons of Japanese ethnicity were forcibly removed from their West Coast homes and incarcerated in camps in remote and desolate areas of the country. Because he was living in Utah as a small child, he did not personally experience the incarceration. He has studied the issue and has written about that period of history and about subsequent happenings within the Asian American community. Some of his work has been published in a book entitled, *The Japanese American Story As Told Through a Collection of Speeches and Articles.*

He has written other books and Kindle ebooks with his wife Irene, including, *Bullying is Not Just a Kids' Problem: It is a Matter of Civil Rights*, *In The Aftermath of the Tsunami: Photos From the Japan Tsunami*, *The Hopelessness of Hate,* and *Seven Suggestions for Successful Living.*

He and his wife have lived in the Washington, D.C. area for over ten years. He has enjoyed photographing the cherry blossoms that are a highlight for the residents and tourists each spring. He may be contacted via email at floydforestt@gmail.com.

Dedicated to everyone who enjoys the Beauty of Nature

CONTENTS

PAGE

About The Author   3

Introduction   6

The Gift of the Cherry Trees   7

The Cherry Blossom Festival   8

The National Japanese American   9
Memorial to Patriotism

Collection of Photos   11

Photos From the Tidal Basin   12

Photos From The National Japanese American Memorial   35

Photos From Potomac Park   45

Photos From The Cherry Blossom Parade   52

Other Cherry Blossom Photos   59

Summary   68

Introduction

One of the major tourist attractions and something that the locals look forward to every year in Washington, D.C. is the arrival of the cherry blossoms. Usually around the end of March to the middle of April, the blossoms are beautiful and in full bloom. Depending on the weather, the blossoms can come a little early or a little later.

Although there are cherry trees in many areas of the city, on many streets and various parks, the main attraction is at the Tidal Basin at the outside edge of the city and by the Potomac River. This destination is a tourist attraction all year as the area houses many of the major monuments in the nation's capital. However, during the cherry blossom season, there are thousands of visitors on most days and millions of visitors in total. The pale pink and white blossoms are a beauty to behold. They greatly enhance the magnificence and majesty of Washington, D.C.

Beautiful cherry blossoms dot the city during the early spring, generally only for a few weeks or less. The blossoms are sometimes shortened by a heavy rainfall, and sometimes they come quite early because of a mild winter. The flowering cherry trees with their beautiful pink and white blossoms are always a thing of beauty.

The information contained in this book is from personal experience, study, and material readily available on the Internet.

The photos were taken at different times of the day and are from different years. Some were taken in the early morning hours, some during the middle of the day, and some at dusk.

Also included in addition to photos at the Tidal Basin are additional photos from the National Japanese American Memorial to Patriotism, Potomac Park, and other items related to the Cherry Blossom Festival.

The Gift of the Cherry Trees

Eliza Ruhamah Scidmore is credited with being an early proponent of planting the Japanese flowering cherry trees along the Potomac River. She returned from her first trip to Japan in 1885 and approached officials with the idea of planting cherry trees along the reclaimed waterfront of the Potomac River. Her idea was not accepted, and it would take some decades before the trees graced the shores of the Potomac. She continued to suggest the proposal for the next 24 years.

In 1906, David Fairchild imported 1,000 cherry trees from Japan and planted them on his property in Chevy Chase, Maryland. The Fairchilds were pleased with the trees and began in 1907 to promote the Japanese flowering cherry trees to be planted around streets in the Washington area. In 1908, Fairchild donated cherry tree saplings to schools in the Washington area to plant on their grounds in observance of Arbor Day.

Scidmore was a friend of the Fairchilds and decided to raise money to buy cherry trees and donate them to the District. She wrote a letter to First Lady Helen Taft, wife of newly elected President Howard Taft, informing her of the plans. The First Lady responded quickly and thanked her for the suggestion. She said she had taken up the matter and was promised the trees.

Jokichi Takamine, the Japanese chemist who discovered adrenaline, was in Washington with Mr. Midzuno, the Japanese Consul to New York City on April 8, 1908. When they were informed of the plan to plant Japanese cherry trees, Takamine asked if Mrs. Taft would accept an additional 2,000 trees. Midzuno said the trees could be given in the name of Tokyo as a gift. The offer of the trees was accepted. The gift of the cherry trees was to be part of an effort to enhance the friendship between the United States and Japan.

The original shipment of trees from Mayor Yukio Ozaki of Tokyo arrived in Washington, D.C. on January 6, 1910, but they were found to be infested with insects and had to be destroyed.

In a ceremony held on March 27, 1912, First Lady Helen Taft and Viscountess Chinda, wife of the Japanese Ambassador, planted the first two of the cherry trees on the north bank of the Tidal Basin. At the end of the ceremony, Mrs. Taft presented Viscountess Chinda with a bouquet of American Beauty roses.

There were 1,800 Japanese flowering cherry trees planted from 1913 to 1920 around the Tidal Basin. Trees of other cherry varieties were planted in East Potomac Park. Additional cherry trees have been given to the United States by Japan, including 3,000 in 1965, which were accepted by Lady Bird Johnson, First Lady and wife of President Lyndon B. Johnson. Many of these trees were planted on the grounds of the Washington Monument.

Subsequent First Ladies have also held ceremonies to plant a cherry tree and have been heavily involved with the cherry blossom activities, including recent First Ladies Laura Bush and Michelle Obama.

The Cherry Blossom Festival

A group of American school children re-enacted the initial planting in 1927. In 1934, the District of Columbia sponsored a three-day celebration of the flowering cherry trees. This began the tradition of holding a Cherry Blossom Festival each year in the nation's capital.

A 300-year-old stone lantern was given to the City of Washington by the Japanese ambassador to commemorate the signing of the 1854 Japan-U.S. Treaty of Amity and Friendship by Commodore Matthew C. Perry. The lighting of the lantern formally opened the Festival for a number of years.

The Cherry Blossom Festival was suspended during World War II and resumed in 1947. In 1948, the Cherry Blossom Princess and U.S. Cherry Blossom Queen programs were started by the National Conference of State Societies (NCSS). The Cherry Blossom Festival was changed to a two-week celebration in 1994.

Many events are held during the Cherry Blossom Festival each spring. It is a period filled with a variety of activities for the entire family. Millions of people have participated.

There is an Opening Ceremony to kick off the festivities with world-renowned performers. A Cherry Blossom parade is held that includes many military groups and bands marching, floats, giant balloons held by dozens of people, and the Cherry Blossom Princesses and Queens.

A family day is presented at the National Building Museum where children can participate in hands-on activities to learn about Japan. There are exciting youth performances for all ages. A popular street fair is held on the weekends.

There are Gala Dinners and various parties such as a Pink Tie Party. A Blossom Kite Festival may be held. Live music and entertainment is provided along with a fireworks show.

The Ambassador and Embassy of Japan hold special events in conjunction with the Cherry Blossom Festival and to honor the Cherry Blossom Princesses and Queens. There are special Japanese cultural performances held at the Kennedy Center and other venues throughout the city.

There are boat rides on the Potomac River and bus tours around the city where the cherry blossoms are highlighted. Several special signature events are held during the two-week period. The Cherry Blossom Festival has something for everyone in addition to the enjoyment of seeing the beautiful flowering cherry trees in full bloom.

The National Japanese American Memorial to Patriotism

Although the beautiful cherry blossoms may be seen at various locations throughout the entire city of Washington, D.C., another tourist destination to see a glorious array of cherry blossoms and to learn about history is the National Japanese American Memorial to Patriotism. Anyone visiting the nation's capital would gain from a visit to the Memorial where the Japanese American history is shared.

The National Japanese American Memorial to Patriotism is located just north of the Capitol near Union Station. It is on a triangular plot bounded by Louisiana Avenue, New Jersey Avenue, and D Street, NW. From the southern tip of the site, you can look southeast on New Jersey Avenue and see the Capitol Building. The National Mall and its museums are to the southwest.

The Memorial was dedicated in 2000, and ownership of the Memorial was transferred to the United States Government in 2002. The National Park Service has the responsibility to maintain the Memorial.

The project for the Memorial was initiated in 1988 by the "Go For Broke" National Veterans Association Foundation. The name of this organization was later changed to the National Japanese American Memorial Foundation (NJAMF). The mission statement of NJAMF is: To tell our story of service and sacrifice in protecting the Constitutional rights of all Americans.

Americans of Japanese heritage have a unique story that includes a gross injustice to them during World War II when Japan was at war with the United States. After the Imperial Navy of Japan bombed Pearl Harbor in the United States territory of Hawaii on December 7, 1941, life became extremely difficult for the Americans of Japanese ancestry and their immigrant parents from Japan. After President Franklin D. Roosevelt signed Executive Order 9066 on February 19, 1942, the Japanese Americans were affected greatly as they were immediately looked upon as the enemy.

Japanese Americans and immigrants living on the west coast of the continental United States were forced to leave their homes and were later incarcerated in camps that had been built in remote and desolate areas of the country. Two thirds of the people were American citizens who were mistreated by their own government as their freedom was taken from them.

Although at first considered as enemy aliens not eligible to serve in the U.S. military after the start of World War II, Japanese American young men were later requested to join and were drafted into the Army. A segregated unit of Japanese Americans was formed. Joined with the 100th Battalion of Japanese Americans from Hawaii, the unit became the 442nd Regimental Combat Team. They served in the European theater. Other Japanese Americans served in the military intelligence service in the Pacific.

These brave and dedicated souls proved their patriotism and loyalty to the United States of America. The National Japanese American Memorial to Patriotism honors those Japanese Americans who endured humiliation and rose above adversity to serve their country during one of this nation's greatest trials.

More than 800 Japanese Americans fought and died in World War II defending the freedoms loved by all Americans. The Memorial has a series of panels that list the names of those who gave the ultimate sacrifice on behalf of their fellow citizens.

The Memorial also commemorates the ten camps in which innocent Americans and immigrants from Japan were unjustly incarcerated during World War II. Each of the ten camps has its name and pertinent information on a panel wall at the Memorial.

The sculpture of the crane entangled in barbed wire signifies the unjust imprisonment of the Japanese American population during World War II.

Meaningful words of leaders from within the Japanese American community are etched in stone at various locations throughout the Memorial. Included are words from Norman Y. Mineta, formerly Secretary of Transportation under President George W. Bush and Secretary of Commerce under President Bill Clinton, as well as a long-time former U.S. Congressman, Mayor of San Jose, California, and respected businessman.

The late Senator from Hawaii, Daniel K. Inouye, and the late Congressman from California, Robert Matsui also have quotes at the Memorial. Also included are words from Norman Mineta's brother in law, Mike M. Masaoka, an early leader within the Japanese American Citizens League (JACL), who is credited with most of the work that was accomplished in the civil rights areas for Japanese Americans and Asian Americans.

The Memorial stands in close proximity to the nation's capitol. It is a Memorial to Patriotism to remember the Japanese American history of patriotism and perseverance for posterity. Japanese Americans want their history to be known so that such a travesty of justice will never again be inflicted upon innocent citizens of the United States of America.

Every year during the Cherry Blossom Festival, NJAMF and partner organizations sponsor a National Cherry Blossom Freedom Walk, which ends at the Memorial. A special program is held to celebrate the patriotism of Japanese Americans and others who worked hard to obtain freedom.

A Collection of Photos

The Tidal Basin

National Japanese American Memorial to Patriotism

Potomac Park

Parade

Other Items

PHOTOS FROM THE TIDAL BASIN AREA

WASHINGTON, D.C.

The Jefferson Memorial

The Washington Monument

Martin Luther King Jr. Memorial

31

Japanese Peace Lantern at the Tidal Basin

PHOTOS FROM THE NATIONAL JAPANESE
AMERICAN MEMORIAL TO PATRIOTISM

WASHINGTON, D.C.

The National Japanese American Memorial to Patriotism

41

PHOTOS OF CHERRY BLOSSOMS

AT POTOMAC PARK

Running a 5K amidst the cherry blossoms

A California family visiting Washington, D.C. and enjoying the cherry blossoms

PHOTOS FROM A

CHERRY BLOSSOM PARADE

WASHINGTON, D.C.

OTHER CHERRY BLOSSOM PHOTOS

A Cherry Blossom Tie

Cherry Blossom Necklaces and Pins

The National Conference of State Societies

THE 2011

CHERRY BLOSSOM
PRINCESS
PROGRAM

About the
CHERRY BLOSSOM
Festival

THE ADVENT OF SPRING IN THE NATION'S CAPITAL brings thousands of admirers to the Tidal Basin, where clouds of pink and white blossoms spill from trees that were donated in the early 20th century as a symbol of friendship between Japan and the United States.

This year, our celebration of the cherry blossom season is tempered by the knowledge that so many are suffering in the aftermath of the multiple disasters that have struck Japan in recent weeks. We keep the Japanese people in our thoughts and prayers.

The connection symbolized by the cherry blossoms dates back to March 27, 1912, when First Lady Mrs. William Howard Taft and Viscountess Chinda, the wife of the Japanese Ambassador, planted the first two trees in West Potomac Park. In the 1920s and 1930s, school groups sponsored a variety of informal cherry blossom ceremonies when the trees were in bloom. By 1939, state societies in Washington were recruiting college students to serve as Cherry Blossom Princesses and to represent their states in festival ceremonies. Since 1948, the National Conference of State Societies has sponsored festival activities every year.

Next year will mark the 100th anniversary of the planting of the two inaugural trees. In the months ahead, we will continue to stand with the resilient Japanese people during their difficult recovery, looking forward in hope to the rebuilding season when the cherry trees bloom again.

Anyone who wishes to help is encouraged to do so through the American Red Cross at http://www.redcross.org/

2011 CHERRY BLOSSOM PRINCESS PROGRAM

The 2011 Cherry Blossom Friendship & Relief Ball
for Japan

Silent Auction Program

Renaissance Washington, DC Hotel

Friday, April 8, 2011

Celebrating the 99th Anniversary

Of the flowering of the Cherry Blossom Trees

In our Nation's Capital

And the 63rd Anniversary of the

Cherry Blossom Princess Program during the

National Conference of State Societies 59th

Anniversary

Saturday April 6, 2013

"Life, Liberty and the pursuit of Justice"

25th anniversary of the civil liberties act of 1988 &
The 15th anniversary of the freedom walk

KEYNOTE SPEAKER: Joan Z. Bernstein
Chair of the commission on the wartime relocation and internment of civilians

National Japanese American Memorial to Patriotism
(New Jersey and Louisiana Avenues and D St., NW –
Closest Metro Union Station)

Check-in opens at 9:00 AM • Opening Ceremony 10:0

Rain or Shine

rs: National Japanese American Memorial Foundation (NJAMF), Japanese American Vet
tion, DC Chapter of the Japanese American Citizens League and Southwest Airlines (t
MF).

NCSS | NATIONAL CONFERENCE *of* STATE SOCIETIES

2016 Japanese Stone Lantern Lighting
Ceremony

Sunday, April 10, 2016

Japanese Stone Lantern Plaza
Tidal Basin

Summary

While Washington, D.C. is a popular tourist destination at any time of the year, it is particularly desirable and beautiful in the spring while the cherry blossoms are in full bloom. Signaling the start of spring, the blooms are generally at their peak around the end of March and the first of April. However, the weather can cause the blossoms to come earlier or later, which may make timing of vacation plans a little difficult.

The cherry trees that were originally a gift from the nation of Japan lend a special grace and beauty to a remarkable city, the nation's capital. The two-week Cherry Blossom Festival held each year offers a variety of activities and events to entertain and delight.

The beauty of the cherry blossoms in the nation's capital rival the popularity of the blooms in Japan where the season of the cherry blossoms is a time of great festivity and happiness.

The blossoms are significant in the remembrance of a unity of spirit and friendship between the two countries of the United States and Japan.

Thank you for your interest in the Cherry Blossoms.

MAY YOU ENJOY THE BEAUTIES OF NATURE.